I Believe God

Book 2

Rev. Dr. Bobby R. Showers, Sr.

BK Royston Publishing
P. O. Box 4321
Jeffersonville, IN 47131 502-802-5385
http://bkroystonpublishing.com

© Copyright – 2017

All Rights Reserved. No part of this book may be reproduced, stored in a retrieval system, or transmitted by any means without the written permission of the author.

Cover Design by: Brent Barnett for besquareddesign.com

ISBN-10: 1-946111-21-X

ISBN-13: 978-1-946111-21-0

Printed in the United States of America

Acknowledgements

First, and foremost I want to thank the Holy Father, by the Son, through the Holy Ghost for saving me and putting me in the ministry. Thanks, be to God for my parents the late Nathaniel L. Showers, Sr. and Arlene M. Showers. My dear mother was saved in the year I was born, 1950.

Special thanks to my extraordinary wife of 44 plus years, our ten children, along with our 14 grandchildren and 1 great grandchild. To my siblings who have been an inspiration to me, especially Dr. Lavanner Brown who encouraged me to enroll in Seminary School.

To the late Rev. T.J. Johnson, the first preacher I knew and who taught and showed me how to live a Christian life. To my pastor since 1972, Rev. Dr. Samuel C. Brown, Sr., pastor of Mt. Vernon Missionary Baptist Church where I preached my first sermon in 1981 and was ordained by Dr. Brown the following year. To the pastor who baptized me, the late Rev. Versey Smith and his nephew, Rev. Frank Baker of St. Mary Baptist Church in Livingston, Louisiana.

Thanks, be to God for my church family who has allowed me to be their pastor: First and foremost, Community Baptist Church of Fluker, Louisiana, where I started in September 1982. Rose Valley Baptist Church, of Roseland, Louisiana, where I have been since March 1988. To Zion Travelers Missionary Baptist Church, of Independence, Louisiana, where I have served as Pastor since August 2011. Special thanks go to Mrs. Sabrina James and Mrs. Lasaundra Pitts for their work and to Mrs. Barbara Hardesty for her untiring labor.

Resume

Rev. Dr. Bobby R. Showers, Sr. 11249 Wardline Rd • Hammond, LA 70401
Phone: (225) 567-5240 • Email: drbrshowers50@yahoo.com

Objective

As 1 Timothy 4:16 states, I will take heed unto myself and unto the doctrine; continuing in them: for in doing this I shall save myself, and them that hear me. For this reason, I will teach and preach no other doctrine.

PERSONAL

Born To the late Nathaniel L. Showers, Sr. and Arlene M. Showers Family: United in Holy Matrimony with Oralean J. Showers on June 30, 1973, unto this union ten talented children were born. They are known as the Showers Family Gospel Singers, who sing God's praises.

MINISTERIAL EXPERIENCE

Preached Initial Sermon   April 1981
Mt. Vernon Baptist Church, Hammond, LA
Dr. Samuel C. Brown, Pastor

Ordained to the Ministry   June 1982
Mt. Vernon Baptist Church, Hammond, LA
Dr. Samuel C. Brown, Pastor

Community Baptist Church - September 1982 – August 2011 Fluker, LA

Rose Valley Baptist Church   March 1988 - Present Roseland, LA

Zion Travelers Missionary Baptist Church   August 2011 to Present Independence, LA

RELIGIOUS POSITIONS

President, Third District   Present
Bogue Chitto Baptist Association

Bible Teacher, Third District   Past
Bogue Chitto Baptist Association
Sunday School – School Congress Ministers Class

Chairman, Third District   Past
Bogue Chitto Baptist Association's
Evangelical Board

First Vice President of the Third District   Past
Bogue Chitto Baptist Association

Recording Secretary,
LA Home & Foreign Mission   Present
Baptist State Convention, Inc.

Assistant Treasurer of N.B.C.A., Inc., Int'l   Present
Board Member of Christian Community Network

Recording Secretary, Tangipahoa Interdenominational Ministers — Past

Elected Sunday School Missionary Hammond, LA — Past

Recording Secretary, Amite River Progressive Christian Association — Past

Recording Secretary, Third District Bogue Chitto Baptist Association — Past

FOUNDATIONS

Founder & Coordinator, Annual Community Revival, Roseland, LA — Present

Coordinator of Joint Fellowship (Four Churches) Roseland, LA — Present

CIVIC POSITIONS

President of CARE (Churches and Responders Engaged)
    Present

Recording Secretary for Home away from home
    Present

Board Member on the WIA Board — Present

Chairperson CNN (Christian Community Network)
Present

EDUCATION

Doctor of Theology Degree,	July 1998
Andersonville Baptist Seminary Camilla, GA	
Master of Theology Degree,	April 1997
Andersonville Baptist Seminary Camilla, GA	

Bachelors of Arts Degree   April 1996
International Bible College Independence, MO

Southeastern Louisiana University   1992-1995
 Hammond, LA

Bible College Degree   May 1990
Lynchburg, VA

Broadcasting School   September 1969
 Houston, TX

West Livingston High School   May 1969
 Livingston, LA

REFERENCE AVAILABLE UPON REQUEST

Table of Contents

Acknowledgments

Resume

Introduction

Chapter 1	His Pre-existence Or To Exist Before	1
Chapter 2	The Pre-Incarnate Christ	11
Chapter 3	Our Lord's Incarnation Or Birth	23
Chapter 4	Why The Lord Jesus was Incarnated	33
Chapter 5	Our Lord's Character	45
Chapter 6	Areas Of Which Our Lord Took Courage	55
Chapter 7	His Love For the World	67
Chapter 8	God's Love	79
Bibliography		92

Introduction

In this ever changing and complex society in which we live right has become wrong, and wrong has become right. Who are we to believe the lawmakers in Washington D.C., our state legislatures, politicians, or will we believe God? What brought about this book, "I Believe God" was the Holy Spirit directing me to do a series of the rightly divided Word of God." It is a sin for anyone to wrongly divide the word. We must follow the Lord's command in II Timothy 2:15. It is my prayer that after you have read this book you will say with the Apostle Paul, "I Believe God." This whole chapter of Acts is given up to the reality of a shipwreck. Paul, a prisoner in chains, was on his way to Rome, to stand before Caesar. The ship in which he was aboard had reached the Fair Havens, a beautiful port where much time was spent. Paul, at this point admonished Julius the centurion and others, saying "Sirs, I perceive that this voyage will be with hurt and much damage, not only of the cargo and ships, but also of our lives. Nevertheless the centurion believed the master and the owner of the ship, more than those things which were spoken by Paul." Isn't that like a lot of folks you know both in sacred, as well as secular history who would rather hear others over the preacher? My brothers and sisters, if the preacher is declaring "Thus saith the Lord," you had better hear him, or he is God's man, in God's place, speaking for God. No doubt the centurion said, "This land lubber of a preacher may do pretty well for a pulpit, but he doesn't know a square yard from a crossjack when it comes to a ship." So he gave command to sail on. Nevertheless, Paul was right and the captain wrong. The text says, "Not long after there arose against the ship a tempestuous wind called Euroclydon, which meant a southeast wind that stirs up waves." The ship was in trouble and the lives of the 276 people that were on board were threatened. "But after long abstinence Paul stood forth in the midst of them, and said, Sirs you should have hearkened unto me, and not have loosed from Crete, and to have gained this harm and loss." Why would Paul talk to the crew this way? Was he being sarcastic? Not at all; for Paul was not taunting them with an "I told you so," but was reminding them that through the leadership of the Holy Spirit, he had predicted this very problem. In the future, they listened to him and their lives were spared according to verses 30-32 of the text. Paul, seeing and knowing the fretfulness of the centurion and others, gave them some good news from the Lord. He said, "And now I exhort you to be of good cheer: "For there stood by me this night the angel of God, whose I am and whom I serve, saying Fear not, Paul; thou must be brought before Caesar, and lo, God hath given thee all them that sail with thee. "What a man this servant of the most High God was, because the Lord spared all the lives aboard the ship because of Paul. Oh friends, think about how many people's lives are still going on, because the Lord had one of his servants aboard. It ought to behoove every sinner to give his or her life to Christ because the Lord has allowed your golden moments to roll on a few days longer because his child interceded on your behalf. Paul, here in verse 25, sets forth a bold statement, "Wherefore, sirs, be of good cheer: for I believe God that it shall be even as it was told me." Those three words, "I believe God," are the words every born again believer ought to say twenty-four hours a day, 365 days a year, and 366 of a leap year. Have you ever pondered and wondered why there is so much trouble in Christendom today? It is simply because we don't believe God. The apostle Paul could say, "Nevertheless, I am not ashamed: For I know in whom I have believed, and am persuaded that he is able to keep that which I have committed unto him against that day." (II Timothy 1:12) Oh in this day and hour, for those of us that are believers in Christ, stand up and say as never before, "I believe God." When the homosexuals and lesbians of our day are marrying each other, we ought to tell them, "I believe God." For God said, "If a man also lies with mankind, as he lieth with a woman, both of them have committed an abomination: they shall surely be put to death; their blood shall be upon them." (Leviticus 20:13) Do you and I believe God about this issue, or the Supreme Court of Massachusetts that made it legal? To make matters worse the United States Supreme Court failed to overturn this ruling, therefore they don't believe God either. Dr. John Rice said, "Never put a question mark where God has put a period." When most Americans think it acceptable to gamble away that which the Lord has graciously blessed them with, I believe God in what he says about the issue. "He that by usury and unjust gain increaseth his substance, he shall gather it for him that will pity the poor." (Proverbs 28:8). "He that maketh haste to be rich shall not be innocent" (Proverbs 28:20) "For the love of money is the root of all evil which while some coveted after, they have pierced themselves through with many sorrows." (I Timothy 6:10). Thou shalt not covet" (Exodus 20:17).Gambling, as someone wrote, is not acting on faith. It is taking an artificial risk for hope of excessive gain far beyond what the investment of time, money or skill would justify. A gamble is a transaction whereby your gain is someone else's loss.

When you gamble, you try to exploit chance; you hope that you will be the only lucky one. So gambling is the opposite of faith.

The Bible says, "The just (Christian) should live by faith." (Galatians 3:11b) Will we believe God on this issue or man?

Another hot topic in our society where we ought to say, "I believe God," is the issue of abortion, which is the killing of innocent babies. You and I both know that it should be "The Lord giveth and the Lord taketh away." (Job 1:21) But man believing in self and not God decides who should live and not die. Man says, "It's not a life until full development." But God told Jeremiah, "Before I formed thee in the belly, I knew you." (Jeremiah 1:5) Also at the moment of conception life begins for the child and the Lord has a record of every child that has been conceived. Oh friends today, don't believe the pro-choice advocate which says, "A woman has the right to choose", but believe God when He says, "Lo children are a heritage of the Lord: and the fruit of the womb is his reward." (Psalms 127:3) In this day and hour like never before, let each of us say, "I believe God." From the Bible, which should be the believer's guide, let each of us say, "I believe God. "It was God's word that spoke it, He took the bread and broke it and with the word did make it, that I believe and take it." DL Wilmington

Chapter 1

His Pre-Existence Or To Exist Before

Introduction:

Here we are again my brothers and sisters on behalf of the Holy Father, to continue what He started us with, a series on, "I Believe God."

Our Heavenly Father's last ten messages through us have been on these three words, "I Believe God." It is not coincidental that these words were spoken by one of the greatest Christians of all time, the Apostle Paul.

What this great man of God spoke to the captain, centurion, crew and others, are words that should be on every Christian's heart and spoken from every Christian's mouth, "I Believe God."

You the members of this church and others have heard about a number of issues in which I have declared that I believe God about.

I've done my best with the Holy Spirit's guide to not give you my own opinion, but what the Bible teaches through rightly dividing it.

On this day, after seeking God's will in this continued series on, "I Believe God", the triune God is leading us to begin a succession of sermons on, "Jesus Christ and The Way He Did Things."

Yes our Lord Jesus Christ is the most important man to tabernacle here on earth. There are a number of things that we as believers ought to know and believe about Him. Also it is a good time for those who are lost to hear about the man who can save our soul from hell's eternal flames.

The first and foremost thing that we will set forth concerning our Lord Jesus Christ is:

His Pre-existence or to Exist Before

> Notice that I did not say His existence of which many of us are aware, because He was born the little babe in Bethlehem.
>
> But what the Lord would have us know is the fact that He existed before His incarnation or birth. "In the beginning was the Word and the Word was with God and the Word was God."(St. John 1:1)
>
> Brothers and sisters I stand in awe of the fact that Jesus Christ has been, is, and will always be. The Lord Jesus proclaimed to the Apostle John on the Isle of Patmos, "I am Alpha and Omega, the first and the last, the beginning and the ending." (Revelation 1:8) To Micah the prophet, the Lord on His preexistence says, "But thou, Bethlehem Ephratah, though thou be little among the thousands of Judah, yet out of thee shall he (The Lord Jesus) come forth unto me that is to be ruler in Israel; whose goings forth have been from old, from everlasting." (Micah 5:2)
>
> In John's gospel in His high priestly prayer, the Lord

said, "And now, O Father, glorify thou me with thine own self with the glory which I had with thee before the world was." (John 17:5)

In John 17:24, The Lord on His preexistence says, "Father, I will that they also, whom thou hast given me, be with me where I am; that they may behold my glory, which thou hast given me: for thou lovedst me before the foundation of the world."

Yes brothers and sisters our Lord Jesus preexisted in spite of what some may think.

Many can believe and will accept as fact that there were prehistoric men as the Cro-Magnon, Javal man, Neanderthal man, which is fictitious, but can't accept the fact of the preexistent Son of God. The Jehovah False Witnesses blatantly declares that our Lord preexisted as Michael the archangel before his arrival or birth at Bethlehem.

There is little wonder that this cult is a branch of false witnesses because the Bible is clear as to the identity of Michael as an angel.

This can be seen in Daniel 10:13; 21;12:1; Revelation 12:7; but the Lord Jesus Christ, with the Father and Holy Spirit created Michael and all the other angels as is set forth by Genesis 2:1; Nehemiah 9:6; Psalm 148:2,5.

The Apostle Paul on our Lord's existence says, "Who is the image of the invisible God, the firstborn (first in rank) of every creature: For by him were all things created, that are in heaven, and that are in earth, visible and invisible, whether they be thrones, or dominions, or principalities, or powers, all things were created by Him, and for Him. And He is before all things and by him all things consist." (Colossians 1:15-17)

As for our Lord's preexistence and the verse of our exposition of Him, let us hear what our Lord told the scribes and Pharisees concerning Himself.

Jesus said unto them, Verily, verily, I say unto you, Before Abraham was, I am." (St. John 8:58) Here the Lord Jesus Christ claims with a double "Amen" "The Incommunicable name, I Am."

Did you hear that declaration of the Lord Jesus? "Before Abraham was, I am." The Lord here to these religious leaders and to each of us is saying "Who told Abram, Get thee out of thy country, and from thy kindred, and from thy father's house, unto a land that I will shew thee." (Genesis 12:1)

Well that was, "I Am." Who was it that told Abraham that Sarah his wife would have a son? That was I Am. Who was that communing with Abraham about the wickedness of Sodom and Gomorrah and its destruction? That was I Am.

Who was it that told Abraham to offer up his son Isaac as a burnt offering and then turned around and provided the ram for one? Again it was I Am.

Who was that which called Moses from the burning bush and then commissioned him to go to Egypt? It was none other than I Am.

Though the religious leader's comprehension of Jesus was shallow, He schooled them on who he was. My Father and I have dual claim to the title, "I AM."

In essence I am what I need to be. "I am the bread of life", "I am the door", "I am the good shepherd", "I am the resurrection and the life", I am the way, the truth, and the life", and "I am the true vine."

Is there anything you and I need Him to be? If so, He stands ready and is wiling right now to be yours and my "I Am."

The Lord is merely saying, "I am the blank for all your needs."

    If you're weak, I am your strength.

    If you're poor, I am your riches.

    If you're sick, I am your health.

    If you're unsaved, I am your salvation.

    If you're in darkness, I am your light.

    If you're in bereavement, I am your comforter.

    If you're in darkness, I am your light.

    If you're homeless, I am your shelter.

> If you're friendless, I am one that sticketh closer than any brother.
>
> Thanks be to God that He is the Great I Am of His Children.

What was the preexistent one setting forth to these religious leaders when He said, "Before Abraham was, I Am?"

He did not mean that he, the human figure Jesus, had always existed. For we know that Jesus was born into the world at Bethlehem, and that there is more than that here.

Let us look at it this way. There is only one person in the universe who is timeless and that one person is God. What Jesus is saying here is nothing less than the life in him is the life of God. The writer of Hebrews set forth, "Jesus Christ, the same yesterday, today, and forever more." (Hebrews 13:8)

In Jesus we see, not simply a man who came and lived and died, we see the timeless God, who was and is the God of Abraham, of Isaac, and of Jacob. He was before time and who will be after time, who always is.

We must believe God first about His preexistence, so we can readily believe in His existence.

Let us examine some of the activities of the preexistent Christ. (1) He was creating the Universe, (2) He was controlling this Universe and (3) He was communing with the Father.

I. He Was Creating The Universe

This universe did not come about as some believe by a cosmic explosion, but it was well thought out and planned.

The Bible says, "In the beginning God created the heaven and the earth." (Genesis 1:1) Also in John's gospel it says, "All things were made by Him; and without Him was not anything made that was made!" (St. John 1:3)

The Lord Jesus Christ the preexistent one was in on all the action of creation.

The Bible does not say that, "He had a part in some of the things of creation, but He was in on it all."

When the Bible says, "Let there be light: and there was light," He was there. When it says, let the firmament be in the midst of the waters, and let it divide the water from the waters," He was there.

Everything that ever was, is, and will ever be, including the creation of man, the preexistent Christ was there.

Not only was the preexistent Christ a part of creating the universe but,

II. He was Controlling This Universe

The things that were created by Him had to be controlled by the same. What the Lord has put in place is still in place as he created it.

The sun that is 93 million miles from the earth remains where it was placed. If it was not, we would all burn up.

Aren't you glad that He is in control of the moon and stars which constantly give us light at night? If the Lord was not in control of them there would be utter darkness.

Thank God for His word that tells us of His being in control. "And He is before all things, and by Him all things consist." (Colossians 1:17).

"Who being the brightness of his glory, and the express image of His person, and upholding all things by the word of his power." (Hebrews 1:3) The Lord's word holds and controls everything in the universe for His honor and glory.

Not only was the preexistent Christ in on the creating of the universe and in on the controlling of it, but finally.

III. He Was Communing With the Father

There has never been or ever will be a communication problem with the Father, Son, and Holy Ghost.

There was perfect communion in the creation process, for it could have been no other way.

The Lord Jesus Christ in His high priestly prayer prayed of that communion which was prevalent before His advent into this world.

"And now, O Father, glorify thou me with thine own self with the glory which I had with thee before the world was." (John 17:5)

In other words, our Lord was saying to His Father, "What honor and glory we enjoyed together before my departure, I want the same now."

What were some of the conversations the Father, Son, and Holy Spirit had during His preexistence?

They conversed about man, for I believe, before God created him that the trinity spoke of the first man Adam, that would be born, and how that man would fail the God that created him.

I believe as the conversation proceeded, that as they knew man would fail, how that the Second Adam, The Lord Jesus Christ, would come and pay the sin debt for what the first man did.

The Bible even says that, "He would be slain before the foundation of the world." (Revelation 13:8)

Conclusion:

How blessed we are to have a Saviour that preexisted and has kept his promise to be with us always to the end of the world.

Thank God that He is the preexisting one, who fulfilled all that He was to do as Lord and Saviour. And He will continue to be everything that we need Him to be.

Because of His preexistence and what He did during His existence I can sing, "There Is A Name I Love To Hear"

1. "There is a name I love to hear, I love to sing its worth. It sounds as music in mine ear, the sweetest name on earth.
"O how I love Jesus, oh how I love Jesus, O how I love Jesus, because he first loved me."

2. "It tells me of a Saviour's love, who died to set me free. It tells me of His precious blood, the sinner's perfect plea."

3. "It tells me what my Father hath in store for every day, and though I tread a darksome path, yields sunshine all the way."

4. "It tells of one whose loving heart can feel my deepest woe, who in each sorrow bears a part, that none can bear below"
"O how I love Jesus, oh how I love Jesus, O how I love Jesus, because he first loved me."

Chapter 2

The Pre-Incarnate Christ

Introduction:

Here again this morning the Holy Father brings us together to hear another discourse on these three words, "I Believe God." These words were spoken by the Apostle Paul after being assured by the Lord that there was no need for him to fear, for he must be brought before Caesar.

In essence the Lord was saying, "I am the reason you are on this ship to Rome and in spite of this great storm, be of good cheer and believe me."

Every now and then the Lord God has to reassure us as He did Paul to continue on believing in Him and not worry or be fretful of our circumstances.

Paul's believing God brought relief to the captain, his crew, the centurion, and the others aboard the ship, just as our believing God ought to do for those around us who seem to be troubled.

Our believing God can and will bring comfort and ease much of the stress and strain that is being experienced in today's society. There was a report in the news stating that it has been discovered that some have aged ten years because of stress.

Brothers and sisters I know it is repetitious, but we must believe God so that our lives can be ones of serenity and not worry.

This God ordained series of messages should enable and help us to accept and appreciate the Lord God who wants us to believe Him.

In our previous messages we have in this succession heard about the many issues of our day, which we ought to believe God about and not man.

In our last message we continued in our studies by setting forth the commencement of a chain of addresses about "Jesus Christ and the way He Did It."

The Lord enabled us to speak about His preexistence. Remember He told the Pharisees, "Before Abraham was I Am." In that message the Lord told us, "I Am what you need me to be." That is that the Lord Jesus Christ was in the beginning. That He is from everlasting to everlasting and also is the Alpha and Omega, the first and the last.

On this wonderful and glorious morning allow me with the Holy Spirit's guide to speak to your heart and mine about the Christophanies of the Old Testament.

That is to say that the Lord Jesus Christ made various appearances in the Old Testament, or that He was on the scene with many characters of the Old Testament before He was born in Bethlehem.

No wonder it has been said that the Old Testament is the New Testament concealed, and the New Testament is the Old Testament revealed. In other words the same Christ that appeared in the Old Testament as, "The Angel of the Lord," is the same one which appeared in the New Testament."

To many the pre-incarnation of Christ is minute, but believe me it is of absolute importance, because it teaches us about our Saviour, who not only cares about us, but man from his inception.

Let us examine the first appearance on earth of the pre-incarnate Christ

I. To Adam and Eve

>Adam and Eve as we know were created by God and placed in the Garden of Eden. They were given an explicit command to not eat of the tree of knowledge of good and evil. For the day that they would eat of it, they would surely die. (Genesis 2:17)

>As we all know they did eat, and their eyes were opened and both realized their nakedness and sewed fig leaves together, and made themselves aprons. (Genesis 3:6-7)

>And they heard the voice of the Lord God walking in the garden in the cool of the day: and Adam and his wife hid themselves from the presence of the Lord God amongst the trees of the garden. And the Lord God called unto Adam, and said unto him, where art thou? Who was this? Let us allow the word of God to tell us. The Bible says, "In the beginning was the Word, and the Word was with God, and the Word was God. The same was in the beginning with God. And the Word was made flesh and dwelt among us, (and we beheld His glory, the glory as of the only begotten of the Father), full of grace and truth." (St.

John 1:1; 14)

So who was that walking in the garden? It was the Word of God, yes, none other than the Christ of God.

It was the Christ which told the serpent, "Because thou hast done this (Beguiled the woman), thou art cursed above all cattle, and above every beast of the field. Upon thy belly shalt thou go, and dust shalt thou eat all the days of thy life! (Genesis 3:14)

And I will put enmity between thee and the woman, and between thy seed and her seed; it shall bruise thy head, and thou shalt bruise His heel." (Genesis 3:15)

This verse is a prophetic utterance of the Christ which spoke to Adam, Eve, and the serpent.

This is the first Christophany in the Old Testament.

II. He Appeared To Hagar

Hagar was the handmaid (maid- servant) of Sarah, the wife of Abraham. Sarah being barren or without child told Abraham to go in unto my maid; it may be that I may obtain children by her.

Abraham hearkened unto Sarah and went in unto Hagar and she conceived. After her conception Sarah was displeased and told Abraham, "My wrong be upon thee: I have given my maid into thy bosom; and when she saw that she had conceived, I was despised in her eyes: the Lord judge between me and thee." (Genesis 16: 2; 3; 4)

Sarah dealt harshly with Hagar and she fled from her face. It was at this time that the Bible says, "And the angel of the Lord found her by a fountain of water in the wilderness, by the fountain in the way to Shur.
And he said, "Hagar, Sarah's maid, whence camest thou? And whither wilt thou go?" And she said, "I flee from the face of my mistress Sarah."

And the angel of the Lord said unto her, "Return to thy mistress, and submit thyself under her hands." And the angel of the Lord said unto her, I will multiply thy seed exceedingly, that it shall not be numbered for multitude.

And the angel of the Lord said unto her, "behold thou art with child, and shalt bear a son, and shalt call his name Ishmael; because the Lord hath heard thy affliction." Ishmael is the forefather of the Arabs. (Genesis 16:7-14)

This angel of the Lord that spoke to Hagar was none other than the Lord Jesus Christ.

So to Hagar we see the second Christophany

III. He appeared to Abraham

In Genesis 18:1-15 the Bible says, "And the Lord appeared unto Abraham in the plains of Mamre: and he sat in the tent door in the heat of the day; And he lift up his eyes and looked and, lo, three men stood by him: and when he saw them he ran to meet them from the tent door, and bowed himself toward the ground.

The three men who appeared to Abraham were the pre-incarnate Christ and two angels. The Lord told Abraham that Sarah his wife would have a son.

He also told Abraham of His intentions to destroy Sodom and Gomorrah. Abraham interceded with the Lord by asking, "Wilt thou also destroy the righteous with the wicked? Abraham as we know was concerned about Lot his nephew that had taken up residence there.

How good it is to know that the Lord spared Lot, his wife, and two daughters, though Mrs. Lot turned into a pillar of salt because she looked back.

I'm sure Abraham could say, "Praise God for the preincarnate Christ. We to ought to be able to say, "O how wonderful, O how marvelous to have Jesus, to have Him live within us."

Friends today, if you don't have Him, call upon Him right now and ask Him to come into your heart, soul, and mind.

If you and I believe God we will accept the validity of the Lord Jesus Christ being pre-incarnate.

Abraham as we have seen had the third Christophany.

IV. He Appeared To Jacob

How wonderful it was for the pre-incarnate Christ to appear to Abraham and then proceed to make himself known unto his grandson.

Yes, He appeared unto Jacob the one which bought his Brother Esau's birthright and then deceived his father Isaac into blessing him rather than Esau.

After Jacob's deception of his father he fled from Canaan and was told by his father to go to Padanaram. There he would meet Laban the brother of his mother Rebekkah.

While en-route to his uncle, the Bible says in Genesis 28: 11-15 that Jacob came upon a certain place and tarried there all night because the sun was set. He took of the stones of that place, and put them for his pillows, and lay down in that place to sleep.

And he (Jacob) dreamed, and behold a ladder set up on the earth, and the top of it reached heaven: and behold the angels of God ascended and descended on it.

And, behold, the Lord stood above it, and said, I am the Lord God of Abraham thy father, and the God of Isaac: the land whereon thy liest; to thee will I give it, and to thy seed.

Who was this that Jacob saw? It was the preincarnate Christ. Also to Jacob the Lord made another exhibition.

Jacob at this time was heading back to Canaan with his wives, children, herd and all. He knew he had to meet Esau and was greatly afraid and distressed according to Genesis 32:7.

The Bible says, "And Jacob was left alone; and there wrestled a man with him until the breaking of the day. And when he saw that he prevailed not against him, he touched the hollow of Jacob's thigh; and the hollow of Jacob's thigh was out of joint, as he wrestled with him.

And he said, "Let me go, for the day breaketh." And he said, "I will not let thee go, except thou bless me." (Genesis 32:24-26)

"And Jacob called the name of the place Peniel: for I have seen God face to face and my life is preserved." (Genesis 32:30)

Again the pre-incarnated Christ made himself known unto Jacob. What a blessed privilege this man of God had in twice seeing the Christ.

V. He Appeared To Moses

Yes Moses the meekest man in the earth had an encounter with the Lord Jesus Christ. Our Lord's appearance unto Moses was at the burning bush.

From that bush the Lord spoke unto Moses his plan for the deliverance of the children of Israel out of Egyptian bondage.

From that burning bush the Lord told Moses, "I Am That I Am."

That same man Moses received the law at Mt. Sinai detailing God's plan for Israel. Every word spoken to Moses came from the Word, who is none other but the Christ of God.

VI. He Appeared To Joshua

Yes Joshua the successor to Moses whom the Lord told, "As I was with Moses, so shall I be with you." (Joshua 1:5)

The Bible records in Joshua 5:13-15, the Lord's appearance to Joshua. "And it came to pass, when Joshua was by Jericho that he lifted up his eyes and looked, and behold, there stood a Man over against him with his sword drawn in his hand: and Joshua went unto Him and said unto Him, Art thou for us, or for our adversaries? And he said nay; but as Captain of the host of the Lord am I now come."

And Joshua fell on his face to the earth, and did worship and said unto Him, What saith my Lord unto His servant? And the Captain of the Lord's host said unto Joshua, Loose thy shoe off thy foot; for the place whereon thy standest is holy. And Joshua did so.

Who was this Captain of the Lord's host? The Christophony of the Old Testament.

VII. He Appeared To Manoah and His Wife

Manoah who was of the tribe of Dan had a wife that was barren and the pre-incarnate Christ appeared to them and said, "They would have a son; and no razor shall come on his head: for the child shall be a Nazarite unto God from the womb: and he shall begin to deliver Israel out of the hand of the Philistines." The child was Samson.

Manoah asked, "What is thy name? And the Angel of the Lord said unto him, why askest thou thus after my name, seeing it is secret?

The word for secret in the text is, "Wonderful", and who else could that be but the Christ who is not only Wonderful, but He is The Counsellor, The Mighty God, The Everlasting Father and The Prince of Peace.

VIII. To Isaiah

Yes Isaiah the son of Amos also saw Him. "In the year that King Uzziah, I saw also the Lord sitting upon a throne high and lifted up, and His train filled the temple. Above it stood the seraphims: each one had six wings; with twain he covered his face, and with twain he covered his feet, and with twain he did fly.

And one cried unto another, and said, "Holy, Holy, Holy, is the Lord of Host: the whole earth is full of His glory. And the posts of the door moved at the voice of Him that cried, and the house was filled with smoke. Then said I, woe in me, for I am undone; because I dwell in the midst of a people of unclean lips: for mine eyes have seen the King, The Lord of Hosts." (Isaiah 6:1-5)

O the great prophet, the prince of the prophets saw the King, The pre-incarnate Christ in all of His glory and splendor.

IX. To Nebuchadnezzar

This great king, whom God set up, saw the Christ who came down in the midst of the fiery furnace with Shadrach, Meshach, and Abednego.

You remember after casting these three boys in the furnace, the king arose in haste, and spoke, and said unto his counselors, "Did not we cast three men bound into the midst of the fire?" They answered and said unto the King, "True O King." He answered and said, "Lo, I see four men loose, walking in the midst of the fire, and they have no hurt; and the form of the fourth is like the Son of God." (Daniel 3:24-25)

Conclusion:

All of the afore mentioned had heaven on earth experiences with the pre-incarnate Christ, who made Himself known to His children at the right time and the right place.

Praise God this morning that we have a Saviour who just didn't appear when He was born in Bethlehem, but as we have seen and heard that through Christophanies, the Old Testament saints had exhibitions of Him.

O friends today, He the Lord Jesus Christ has come to earth, suffered, bled, died, and rose again that all which believe in Him can have life, and have it more abundantly.

To those of you that are lost, can't you hear the Saviour calling? Why don't you answer and come to Him right now.

Chapter 3

Our Lord's Incarnation Or Birth

Introduction:

The words of our text were spoken by an extraordinary individual, namely the Apostle Paul. You and I must notice that he did not say, "We believe God, but that "I Believe God."

Brothers and sisters as it was with Paul, so is it with us, that it is an individual thing about our believing God.

As much as I love my wife, children, grandchildren, siblings, you the members of this church and others, yet I can't believe God for you. There are a number of things I can do for you, but I can't believe God for you.

The world doesn't need any more political activists, but it does need more individuals that believe God. Is it an unusual or hard thing to believe God? No, my friends, it is just a matter of you and me taking God at His word.

In our past messages I have set forth to you a number of things I believe about God. The past two dissertations have been about Jesus Christ and the way He did things.

The first message about the Christ was concerning His pre-existence. The last one was about the Christophanies of the Old Testament, or the pre-incarnate

Christ. That is that the Lord Jesus Christ made a number of appearances to many of the characters in the Old Testament.

He appeared to Hagar the maid servant of Sarah, to Abraham as he sat in the door of his tent, to Jacob and gave him a name change to Israel, to Moses, Joshua, Manoah the father of Samson, Isaiah and Nebuchadnezzar to name some. This discourse concerns our Lord's incarnation or birth.

I. Some Prophecies Concerning It

> The first prophetic utterance of the Saviour's birth is Genesis 3:15, "I will put enmity between thee and the woman, and between thy seed and her seed; it shall bruise thy head, and thou shalt bruise his heel."

> This verse sets forth the first glimpse of the gospel (Proto-evangelism). It sets forth three divine truths. (1) That Satan is the enemy of the human race explaining why God put enmity (related to the word enemy) between thee (Satan) and the woman; (2) That He would place a spiritual barrier between thy seed (Satan's people) and her seed (God's people); and (3) That the representative seed of the woman (A human being: Christ) would deliver the death blow to Satan, but in so doing would be bruised Himself. It (or, He) shall bruise (Literally crush) thy head, but thou shalt bruise his head refers to Christ's bruising on the cross, which led to the eventual crushing of Satan and his kingdom. So first of all concerning our Lord's incarnation, we see Him depicted as, "The seed of the Woman."

Secondly, we can see the coming Saviour in His promise to Abram. After Abram was told to get out of Ur of the Chaldees the Lord said to him, And I make of thee a great nation, and I will bless thee, and make thy name great; and thou shalt be a blessing. And I will bless them that bless thee, and curse him that curseth thee: and in thee shall all families of the earth be blessed." (Genesis 12: 1-3)

How would all the families of the earth be blessed? We're blessed by the incarnation or the coming birth of our Lord Jesus Christ.

Though Abraham was a Jew; yet, the Lord promised that salvation would come to the Gentiles through his seed. How amazing it is that the Lord would include all mankind in His birth.

No wonder the Bible says, "For God so loved the world, that He gave His only begotten Son, that whosoever believeth in Him shall not perish, but have everlasting life." (St. John 3:16)

So the Lord's intention in calling Abraham out of his country was for the good of all that would accept Him, whether black or white, rich or poor, bond or free.

Thirdly, the incarnation or birth of the Saviour was seen by the great patriarch Jacob. Though he was in his final hours on earth, he called all his sons who gathered around him and heard him say of the things which would befall each of them.

To Judah, Jacob prophetically said, "The Scepter shall not depart from Judah, nor a lawgiver from between his feet, until Shiloh come; and unto Him shall the gathering of the people be." (Genesis 49:10)

The scepter was a symbol of royal power. Shiloh is a hidden name for Messiah; it is made up of three grammatical parts (sh-l- òh) meaning "Him to Whom the Scepter or Kingdom Belongs."

The (sh) is the relative pronoun, the (l) is the possessive and the òh is the pronominal suffix.

The phrase, "And unto Him shall the gathering of the people be", that is, "And unto Him shall be the obedience of the peoples."

There is a song that is sung in religious circles, "Everything that happened to me that was good God did it, O yes He did. Well friends today, the Lord did what was good in being the Scepter that did not depart from Judah, until He came. Thanks be to God for Shiloh who was incarnated.

To Balaam the one whom Balak tried to get to curse Israel, this prophecy of the coming Messiah was uttered, "I shall see Him, but not now, I shall behold him, but not nigh: there shall come a Star (The Lord Jesus) out of Jacob, and a Scepter shall rise out of Israel, and shall smite the corners of Moab, and destroy all the children of Sheth." (Numbers 24:17)

Yes Balaam by the Holy Spirit says of the incarnate Christ, that He would be the Star of Jacob.

To Moses the man whom God used to deliver his people out of Egypt, the Bible says in Deuteronomy 18:15, "The Lord thy God will raise up unto thee a Prophet from the midst of thee of thy brethren, like unto me; unto him ye shall hearken."

Who was this prophet Moses was speaking that would be raised up? Was it Jeremiah, Isaiah, Ezekiel, Daniel, Hosea, Micah, Nahum, or Zechariah?

No it was the Lord Jesus Christ whom Moses knew would come and do all that the Holy Father commanded Him to do. What a prophet the Lord Jesus was in that He was and is still the Prophet of all Prophets. The Psalmist said of the Lord's incarnation, "Then said I, lo I come in the volume of the book it is written of me. I delight to do thy will O God." (Psalm 40: 7-8)

To Isaiah, known as the prince of the prophets, the Holy Spirit gave him a number of prophecies concerning the incarnate Christ. "There shall come forth a rod out of the stem of Jesse, and a Branch shall grow out of his roots." (Isaiah 11:1)

In Isaiah 7:14, the Bible says, "Therefore the Lord Himself shall give you a sign; Behold, a virgin shall conceive, and bear a son, and shall call his name Immanuel or literally God with us.

O brothers and sisters I stand in awe today and just imagine the astonishment of Mary to conceive God in her womb, carry Him around and hold Him in her hands, feed Him, clothe and shelter Him.

Mary and her husband Joseph went to sleep nightly with God and each morning they arose to see Him. Friends today, again they had God with them in the person of our Lord Jesus Christ. Again He was Immanuel that was born.

In Isaiah's other prophecy of the incarnate Christ, the scripture says, "For unto us a child is born, unto us a son is given: and the government shall be upon His shoulder: and his name shall be called Wonderful, Counselor, The Mighty God, The Everlasting Father, The Prince of Peace. Of the increase of his government and peace there shall be no end, upon the throne of David, and upon his kingdom, to order it, and to establish it with judgment and with justice from henceforth even forever. The zeal of the Lord of hosts will perform this." (Isaiah 9:6-7)

In this passage our Lord is the Gift Child and the prophet Isaiah sees Him as though He were already born. Wonderful, Counselor (pele'yò 'éts) is actually one term in the Hebrew language. A wonder is indicative of a miracle. Counselor is often used in parallel with king.

Thus miraculous counsel is given by this God-like King. The Mighty God (El Gisòr) is the strongest of these titles. In Isaiah, El is always used of God and never refers to man. Gibor means "Hero.

Together El Gibor describes one who is indeed God himself. The question I pose to you is, "Is the Mighty God your hero."

He is also "The Everlasting Father" (abì 'ad) literally means He is the Father of Eternity. This sets Him forth as the one who inhabits and possesses eternity and He is loving, tender, compassionate, an all wise instructor, trainer, and provider. The name Everlasting Father also expresses Christ's fatherly care. This title for the Christ is not in conflict with that of the first person of the Trinity.

Jesus the same little babe born in Bethlehem told Philip, "He that hath seen me hath seen the Father." (St. John 14:9)

The Incarnate Christ is, "The Prince of Peace" (Sar-Shalom) the one who brings peace in the fullest sense of wholeness prosperity, and tranquility.

Each of us can know His peace. The Bible says, "For He (Jesus) is our peace." (Ephesians 2:14)

What a portrayal the prophet Isaiah gave of the coming Saviour, who would be all that the believers in Christ would ever need.

Someone used to sing, "I found all, all that I need, I found it in the Lord."

The next prophetic utterance of the incarnate Christ is given by Jeremiah, known as the weeping prophet.

Hear what is said in Jeremiah 31:22b, "For the Lord hath created a new thing in the earth, a woman shall compass a man."

Though there have been numerous interpretations of what this verse sets forth, I believe God wants us to see primarily of it speaking about the incarnation of Christ.

For in believing God and the Holy Scriptures; we know that Mary <u>compassed</u> Joseph, or went around him and was conceived by the Holy Ghost. Yes the Lord did it without the aid of mortal man.

The prophet Micah received a revelation of the incarnate Son of God and where He would be born. "But thou, Bethlehem Ephratah, though thou be little among the thousands of Judah, yet out of thee shall He come forth unto me that is to be ruler in Israel; whose goings forth have been from of old, from everlasting." (Micah 5:2)

It was no accident that Joseph and Mary went to Bethlehem at the time of the world being taxed. It was in the providence of God that they would be there for the birth of Christ.

In the New Testament there were quite a few who told about the incarnation. We know first of all that the angel Gabriel gave Mary the word of her conceiving the Christ child.

Joseph as we know secondly was contemplating on what to do with Mary who was with child and the Bible says, "But while he thought on these things, behold, the angel of the Lord appeared unto him in a dream saying Joseph, thou son of David, fear not to take unto thee Mary thy wife: for that which is conceived in her is of the Holy Ghost.

"And she shall bring forth a son, and thou shalt call his name Jesus: for He shall save His people from their sins." (Matthew 1:20-21)

To the shepherds out there on the Judean hills the Bible says, "And the angel of the Lord said unto them Fear not: for behold, I bring you good tidings, of great joy, which shall be to all people. For unto you is born this day in the City of David a Saviour which is Christ the Lord. And you shall find the babe wrapped in swabbing clothes, lying in a manager." (Luke 2:10-12)

To the Wise Men it is said, "Now when Jesus was born in Bethlehem of Judea in the days of Herod the king, behold there came Wise men from the east to Jerusalem saying, "Where is He that is born king of the Jews? For we have seen his star in the east, and are come to worship Him. (Matthew 2:1-2)

The man Simeon was promised by God that he would not see death before he had seen the Lord's Christ.

After seeing the Christ, the old man took up the child in his arms, and blessed God, and said, Lord, now lettest thou thy servant depart in peace, according to thy word: For mine eyes have seen thy salvation, which thou hast prepared before the face of all people; a light to lighten the Gentiles and the glory of thy people Israel." (St. Luke 2:25-32)

Conclusion:

O what a relief I'm sure it was to those prophets of old to utter of the coming Saviour. Also those of the New Testament, who witnessed the birth of the only begotten Son of God.

Thanks be to God for our Lord's incarnation, for had he not been born, He could not have died for our sins. For God hath made Him (Jesus) sin for us, who knew no sin, that we might be made the righteousness of God in Him." (II Corinthians 5:21)

We were all made righteous through the shed blood of Jesus on the cross. What can wash away my sins, what can make me whole again? Nothing but the blood of Jesus.

Chapter 4

Why The Lord Jesus Was Incarnated

Introduction:

The Lord once again brings us to this divine moment, whereby we must stand and proclaim His name one more time.

In our proclamation of Him, there must be some belief in Him. At this time of the year being Christmas, how wonderful it would be if everyone who says, "I am in the Christmas spirit," would only believe the Christ, and then they would know what it is all about.

I am afraid today brothers and sisters that there are not enough of us that really believe God about this holiday of Christmas.

We think of it as a joyous time to share with others once a year. But do take it to heart when I say that if you and I believe God, our sharing with each other will be a life time thing.

The man of our text, The Apostle Paul, did not wait until this tempestuous storm Euroclydon came to believe God. But he believed Him before he boarded the ship to Rome.

Let us and I mean each of us, forget about what we may receive or not receive at this time of season, but get these three words, "I Believe God," down in our hearts, soul and mind. Our past three messages in this continued series on "I

Believe God" has been about, "Jesus Christ And the Way He Did It."

We have set forth to you about our Lord's preexistence, His pre-incarnation, and our last message was on His in-carnation or that the Christ was made flesh by being born in Bethlehem of Judaea.

This morning's discourse will be centered around, "Why was Jesus Christ incarnated?"

The Bible that you and I read says, "To everything, there is a season, and a time to every purpose under the heaven: A time to be born and a time to die; a time to plant, and a time to pluck up that which is planted; etc. (Ecclesiastes 3:1-8)

That is to say that the Lord God of Abraham, Isaac, and Jacob had it all planned for the incarnation of His only begotten Son. And there was nothing, the Devil and all of His demons could do to thwart our Father's plan.

You and I must believe God that if there was anything that Satan could have done, he would have, but praise God as the Bible sets forth, "But when the fullness of the time was come, God sent forth His Son, made of a woman, made under the law, to redeem them that were under the law, that we might receive the adoption of sons." (Galatians 4: 4-5).

This verse of scripture along with a number of others sets forth the incarnation of the Son of God. Why would the Heavenly Father go to such great length to do such a thing?

In my believing God allow me to set forth some Biblical reasons why the Lord Jesus was incarnated.

I. To Save Mankind From His Sins

> Yes brothers and sisters that was His primary reason for being incarnated. The Lord God had appeared unto Joseph who was contemplating on whether or not to put Mary away privately.

> "But while he thought on these things, behold the angel of the Lord appeared unto him in a dream, saying, Joseph, thou Son of David, fear not to take unto thee Mary thy wife: for that which is conceived in her is of the Holy Spirit."

> And she shall bring forth a son, and thou shalt call His name Jesus: for He shall save His people from their sins." (St. Matthew 1:20-21)

> Why is He coming? To save His people from their sins. Also the Lord Jesus made known to a man whom He had called down from a sycamore tree name Zacchaeus, why He came into the world. He said to this tax collector, "For the Son of man is come to seek and to save that which is lost." (Luke 19:10)

> Also the same Jesus made known to a Pharisee named Nicodemus, why He had come. Hear the Lord Jesus as He says, "For God sent not His Son into the world to condemn the world; but that the world through Him might be saved." (St. John 3:17)

Three times we see from the Holy Writ the primary reason why our Lord Jesus was incarnated.

II. To Reveal The Invisible God

Yes the invisible God was manifested in the person of our Lord Jesus Christ. The Bible says, "No man hath seen God at any time; the only begotten Son, which is in the bosom of the Father, he hath declared him." (John 1:18)

The Lord Jesus Christ set forth to Philip one of the twelve apostles about Him being the invisible God. Jesus had said, "If ye had known me, ye should have known my Father also: and from henceforth ye know Him, and have seen Him. Philip saith unto Jesus, Lord shew us the Father, and it sufficeth us. Jesus saith unto him, have I been so long time with you, and yet hast thou not known me, Phillip? He that hath seen me hath seen the Father; and how sayest thou then, shew us the Father." (John 14:7-9)

The Lord Jesus in this same book of John declared also, "And he that seeth me seeth Him that sent me." (John 14:45)

Also concerning Jesus and His revelation as the invisible God, hear what Colossians 1:15 says, "Who is the image of the invisible God, the firstborn of every creature."

The Hebrew writer sets forth the same idea of the invisible God. "God who at sundry times and in divers manners spake in time past unto the fathers by the prophets, Hath in these last days spoken unto us by His Son, whom He hath appointed heir of all things, by whom also He made the world, who being in the brightness of His glory, and the express image of His person, and upholding all things by the word of His power, when He had by Himself purged our sins, sat down on the right hand of the Majesty on High." (Hebrews 1:1-3)

Who was, is, and will always be the express image of the Father's person and who was the brightness of His glory, nobody but the Lord Jesus who was revealed as the invisible God.

So secondly, the Lord Jesus came to reveal Himself as the invisible God.

III. To Fulfill Prophecy

Yes the Lord had to come in His incarnation to solidify the saying of Him in the Old Testament.

He had to fulfil Genesis 3:15 as the Seed of the Woman. He had to fulfill Genesis 49:10. Also to accomplish what Balaam said of Him as, "The Star of Jacob."

He had to comply with Isaiah 7:14; 9:6-7 and other prophecies concerning Him.

The Lord did everything He had to do to prove the validity of the Holy Scriptures that they are true from Genesis to Revelation rightly divided.

The Lord had to show man that He was not a God of lies, but one of truth. Thanks be to God that His truth is still marching on in spite of the skeptics.

Yes our Lord had to be incarnated to fulfil the prophecies that had been spoken of Him.

Thanks be to God that the prophecies of Him came to past, unlike many of the false ones that have been around as long as the true ones.

To every good thing the Lord sets forth, the Devil comes along with a counterfeit to try and imitate. Though the Devil got very busy to hinder the fulfillment of prophecy concerning our Lord's incarnation, but He could not thwart the plans of the Lord God of Abraham, Isaac, and Jacob.

There is not a power on earth nor heaven that can bottleneck the plan of God. Everything about the Lord's coming birth at Bethlehem was according to His arrangement. What each of us should gather from this is "We can't beat him, so why not join him. So our Lord's incarnation went according as it was prophesied.

IV. To Provide An Example For Believers

> Yes the Lord Jesus was incarnated (1) To save man from his sins, (2) To reveal the invisible God, and (3) To Fulfil prophecy. But my brothers and sisters, He also came to be a model for us.

There is much talk, teaching, and preaching concerning what we as Christians ought to believe and I dare not minimize it. But believe me, our Lord Jesus was the greatest teacher and preacher, but he also was the greatest example.

He did not come friends just to tell us what we should and ought not do, but to show us through His life how we must be.

Jesus said, "As long as I am in the world I am the light of the world." (John 9:5) That is you never have to fret nor worry about my light ever getting dark or dim.

Friends on this day, that same Jesus expects the same of you and me. The light He gave us at salvation should remain bright until He calls us home.

Our mindset ought to be, "Lord you gave me the light and I am going to let it shine for better or for worse." After all you told me, "I am the light of the world. A city that is set on a hill cannot be hidden.

Let my light so shine before men, that they may see my good works and glorify the Father which is in heaven." (Matthew 5:14, 16)

As our Lord shined before men and they saw His good works, so must we do the same. After all He is our primary example and wants us to mimic Him in our daily walk. The Lord as never before, wants you and me to be copycats.

Young boys and girls quit copying the rap stars, athletes, the dress codes of the world, the bad language, and copy the Lord Jesus and those who follow in His steps.

Those of us that have some years behind us, let us give these young people something to copy. Each of us ought to tell our children, grandchildren and other youth, be my copycat.

The Apostle Paul told the believers at Corinth, "Be ye followers of me, even as I am of Christ." (I Corinthians 11: 1)

My brothers and sisters I can say this day likewise, "Follow me as I follow Christ. As I live, so ought you, as I give my tithes and offerings, so ought you; as I love, so ought you.

My life is not worth living if I can't be a good example to my wife, family and those to whom I minister to. The Lord Jesus again came to this world to be an example.

V. To Destroy The Devil And His Works

> Yes brothers and sisters He came also for that purpose. The Devil has been as a roaring lion since the Lord threw him out of glory.
>
> But one day soon the Devil and all his demons according to the Bible will be cast into the lake of fire.
>
> That is a certainty from the one who became flesh and dwelt among men and women. Yes friends the Devil is loose, but praise God He will be bound.
>
> Hear the words of the Lord Jesus, "I am He that liveth, and was dead, and behold I am alive forever more. Amen; and have the keys of hell and death." (Revelation 1:18) Believe the Lord who came that the Devil is doomed.
>
> So our Lord Jesus came to destroy the Devil and His works.
>
> Finally the Lord Jesus Christ was incarnated

VI. To Provide The Believers With A High Priest.

> As believers in the Lord Jesus Christ, O how we thank Him for coming to save us from our sins, to reveal himself as the invisible God, to fulfil prophecy, to be our example and to destroy the Devil and His works, but praise God every day that He came to be our high priest.
>
> What would the believer's life in Christ be without

Him being our High Priest? Praise God that He met all the qualifications to be so.

The Bible says, "Wherefore, holy brethren, partakers of the heavenly calling, consider the Apostle and High Priest of our profession, Christ Jesus." (Hebrews 3:1)

Yes, let us consider the fact that the Lord Jesus gave us a heavenly calling when we were called out of darkness into His marvelous light.

We are now spiritually in heavenly places with Christ Jesus, but physically we remain on earth and need Him to intercede on our behalf.

The Bible says, "And He that searcheth the hearts knoweth what is the mind of the Spirit, because He maketh intercession for the saints according to the will of God." (Romans 8:27)

Our high priest knows our every sickness and disease before we ever pray about them and stands ready to hear our every cry and pity our every groan.

He again knows and I am glad that He knows all about us.

For we have not a high priest which cannot be touched with the feeling of our infirmities; but was in all points tempted as we are, yet without sin." (Hebrews 4:15)

Yes He is (Our High Priest Jesus) touched every time we groan and mourn. I am so glad today that He knows the meaning of every one of them.

Conclusion:

Thanks be to the Father, Son and Holy Ghost for the incarnation of the Christ and the reason why He was incarnated. It solidifies the fact that our God is an awesome God and that He reigns from heaven above.

Our God as the song says, "A God of Mercy, God of Grace."

"God of mercy, God of grace, Show the brightness of thy face; Shine upon us Saviour, shine, Fill thy church with light divine."

That is what our Lord has done, is doing, and will continue to do, for He is the one that paid it all for us, and all to Him we owe. For sin had left us with a crimson stain; but He washed us white as snow.

Chapter 5

Our Lord's Character

Introduction:

O how wonderful, O how marvelous to have Jesus, to have Him live within. Seeing and knowing this stupendous fact of having the Lord within us, it should behoove us all to say, "I Believe God."

I believe Him because can't no one else do us like He has done, is doing, and will continue do. Knowing the continuity of His love to me, as well as you, there should be no bugaboo about us believing God.

I stand before the Holy Father, His Son, and the Holy Ghost to continue what I started by, persevering with these three words, "I Believe God."

As we embarked upon this series of messages which, I thank the Lord through the Holy Spirit for each dissertation He has given me.

I had no idea when the Lord started us in the Book of Acts that I would still be in the same book, but for some reason, when He brought me to Acts 27:25, I haven't been able to move forward. The reason being is because the God of Abraham, Isaac, and Jacob wanted and still wants us as believers in Christ to forge ahead in our belief in God.

In the previous sequence of messages, the Lord shared with me that I must tell you about gambling, taboos , worldly dancing, women preachers, abortions, marriage part one and two, homosexuality and lesbianism, salvation, hell, the second coming of our Lord, giving, divine healing, alcohol, spiritual renewal, The K. J. V. Bible, capital punishment, civil government, Christian education.

In our last four messages the focus has been on Jesus Christ and The Way He Did It.

Our discussion has been on His pre-existence, His pre- incarnation, His incarnation, and why was He incarnated?

The Lord's directive to me to you on this occasion is His Character. In the message to come we will concentrate on various aspects of our Lord's character.

First and foremost let us define character. Simply put it is a distinguishing feature or to recognize as being different.

Character is made by many acts; it may be lost by a single one. Character is what you are in the dark. ---D. L. Moody

There never has been nor ever will there ever be one like the lowly Jesus, for He stands alone in character and expects us as His children to be a peculiar people, whom He has called out of darkness into His marvelous light.

Concerning character Henry Hancock said and I quote, "Out of our beliefs are born deeds, out of our deeds we form habits; out of our habits grows our character; and on our character we build our destiny."

The greatest college basketball coach of all time, John Wooden said, "Be more concerned with your character than with your reputation, because your character is what you really are, while your reputation is merely what others think you are." Henry W. Beecher said, "He is rich or poor according to what he is, not according to what he has."

Both of these quotes in a nutshell sum up what our Lord was about. His character built Him a destiny which will always stand and there is no doubt His character was wrapped up in doing what pleased His Father.

That in itself is a message for us all to never try and build a reputation of self, but build your character to the satisfaction of the Lord and not men.

The first aspect of our Lord's character we will take aim at will be

I. His Compassion For The Lost

>Was there ever or will there ever be another as compassionate as our Saviour, Jesus Christ. The Bible says, "But when he saw the multitudes, he was moved with compassion on them, because they fainted, and were scattered abroad as sheep having no shepherd." (Matt. 9:36)

>The word in its Greek-English original is esplagchnisthe (es-plangkh-ni-sthee) to be moved inwardly; to yearn with tender mercy, affection, pity, and empathy.

It is the deepest movement of emotions possible, being touched with the deepest feelings possible.

The Bible says, and I quote, "For the word of God is quick, and powerful, and sharper than any two edged sword, piercing even to the dividing asunder of soul and spirit, and of the joints and marrow, and is a discerner of the thoughts and intents of the heart." (Hebrews 4:12)

As our Lord was, so must we be. Compassion on our part should not be for a season, but at all times. For there is always one, that needs our help and attention. Failure on our part to not show forth compassion on others will cause the Lord to frown upon us.

The Bible says, "Whoso stoppeth his ears at the cry of the poor, he also shall cry himself, but shall not be heard." (Proverbs 21:13)

Our Lord and Saviour is setting forth to us that our character should mimic His when it comes to compassion. Our Lord's view was "For the Son of man is come to seek and to save that which was lost." (Luke 19:10) And, the greatest commission given is in all four gospels and in Act 1:8 is "But ye shall receive power, after that the Holy Ghost is come upon you: and ye shall be witnesses unto me both in Jerusalem, and in all Judaea, and in Samaria, and unto the uttermost part of the earth."

How do we view the lost? Should they fend for themselves, or will we be moved enough to tell them about the somebody who can save anybody.

Arthur H. Stainback said, "The value of compassion cannot be over-emphasized. Anyone can criticize. It takes a true believer to be compassionate. No greater burden can be borne by an individual than to know that no one cares or understands."

Do we care? Then show it and not talk it, for talk is cheap, but compassion carries with it a price. The price to be paid by us is the action we take.

Someone may be asking, "How much compassion should I have? The answer is as much as is necessary. There was no limit to our Lord's, so must there not be to ours."

Of our Lord's character as exemplified in His compassion for the lost multitude, He also had it in other areas of His ministry.

II. He Had Compassion Upon The Sick

> The Bible says, "And Jesus went forth, and saw a great multitude, and was moved with compassion toward them and He healed their sick." (Matt. 14:14)

Are we moved when we see folk sick? Does it break our heart as it did the Lord for mankind to be in that predicament? Well friends it ought to, especially when we know it's one that is faithful to the Lord and His work.

How moved I am to see faithful brothers and sisters continue to minister in spite of their limited abilities.

Am I the only one? Not so, for I believe that each of us that name the name of Christ has to be compassionate about them as well as others.

The Holy Father expects His children to feel one another's care and to pray for their recovery. The Bible says, "Bear one another's burdens, and so fulfill the law of Christ." (Galatians 6:2)

That is our part as believers, for our compassion toward others is healing within itself. For all that, many need to know that others care and are concerned about them.

For I know that none of us are foolish enough to think that the Lord will heal everybody, for it was not so in Biblical times, nor in this day.

I have witnessed the healing of some through prayer, but it is brutish for me to believe that all will be healed.

The Apostle Paul, the greatest Christian since Jesus Christ, was sick and you Bible readers know that the Lord did not heal him.

But what our Lord did do to show His compassion was to tell him "My grace is sufficient, my strength is made perfect in weakness."

Paul after witnessing the Lord's compassion said, "Therefore most gladly, I will rather boast in my infirmities, that the power of Christ may rest upon me. Therefore I take pleasure in infirmities, in reproaches, in needs, in persecutions, in distresses, for Christ's sake. For when I am weak, then am I strong." (II Corinthians 12:9-10)

O friends, let us believe God and know that he is still compassionate toward us, whether we get healed or not.

III. He Had Compassion On The Hungry

Yes our Lord's character was set forth in his care and concern for the hungry. The Bible says, "Then Jesus called his disciples unto him, and said, I have compassion on the multitude because they continue with me now three days, and have nothing to eat: and I will not send them away fasting, lest they faint in the way." (St. Matthew 15:32)

Yes the hungry was then and there are still some, not only in foreign fields like Sudan, Ethiopia, Haiti, and other places, not to mention right here in America with all of our resources. As believers in Christ, our compassion must also be towards the hungry. That's why it is so important for us to support missions in our local churches, who can send it to state missions and from there to national and international ones. Though it is commendable for us to support missions, let us keep a watchful eye for those in our midst, and are around us.

Remember the words of the Lord Jesus as He spoke of the time, "When the Son of Man comes in His glory and all the nations will be gathered before Him and He will separate them one from another, as a shepherd divides his sheep from the goats." And He will set the sheep on His right hand, but the goats on the left." (Matthew 25:21-33)

The Lord is not gathering them to find out what kind of home that they lived in; nor the kind of car they rode in, or how much money they had in the bank, but He will want to know, "When I was hungry, did you feed me? When I was thirsty, did you give me to drink? When I was sick, did you visit me, when I was naked, did you clothe me, or did you come see me in prison?" We will want to know, "Lord when did we see you hungry, naked, sick, thirsty or in prison? He will say, "When you saw the least of my brethren in that way, it was me."

IV. He Had Compassion on a Demonic Brother

Yes finally our Lord had compassion on a demon possessed man. The Bible says, "How this man had his dwelling among the tombs, and no man could bind him, no not with chains. Always night and day, he was in the mountains, and in the tombs, crying and cutting himself with stones." (Mark 5:3-5)

The demons within this brother cried with a loud voice, "What have I to do with thee Jesus, thou Son of the Most High God? I adjure thee by God, that thou torment me not. Jesus said unto him, come out of the man, thou unclean spirit." (Mark 5:7-8)

After casting out the demons the man wanted to follow Jesus, but hear what the Bible says, "Howbeit

Jesus suffered him not (Or did not allow him), but saith unto him, go home to thy friends, and tell them how great things the Lord hath done for thee, and hath had compassion on thee." (Mark 5:19)

It did not take a sinner long to know that, while Jesus hated sin, yet He loved the sinner.

What a lesson in compassion for each of us that is in the body of Christ. As Our Lord demonstrated it towards this demon possessed man, so much we have compassion on the alcoholics, drug addicts and many others.

We must never forget that the Lord, put somebody in each of our way, to have compassion on us that we would be what we are in Christ.

None of us can stick out our chest and look down on no one as the Pharisee did the publican in Luke 18:10-14. But all of us were either liars, fornicators, idolaters, thieves, drunkards, drug addicts, etc., but by the grace of God we are what we are in Christ.

As Paul through divine inspiration told the church at Corinth, "And such were some of you; but ye are washed, but ye are sanctified, but ye are justified in the name of the Lord Jesus, and by the Spirit of our God." (I Cor. 6:11)

Praise be to the Father, Son, and Holy Ghost for the compassion bestowed upon us and I believe God that He wants the same of you and I.

Conclusion:

Let us who have received compassion allow the world to know through the song, "What A friend We Have In Jesus"

> "What a Friend we have in Jesus. All our sins and grief's to bear! What a privilege to carry. Everything to God in prayer! O what peace we often forfeit, O what needless pain we bear. All because we do not carry everything to God in prayer."

> "Have we trials and temptations? Is there trouble anywhere? We should never be discouraged. Take it to the Lord in prayer. Can we find a friend so faithful? Who will all our sorrows share? Jesus knows our every weakness. Take it to the Lord in prayer."

> "Are we weak and heavy laden, cumbered with a load of care? Precious Savior, still our refuge, take it to the Lord in prayer. Do thy friends despise, forsake thee? Take it to the Lord in prayer. In His arms He'll take and shield thee. Thou wilt find a solace there."
> Joseph M. Scriven

> Thank God through His Son, by the Holy Ghost for His character shown by His compassion.

Chapter 6

Areas Of Which Our Lord Took Courage

Introduction:

One more time our blessed Lord brings us together for another discourse on these words, "I Believe God."

If they are not the heart beat of every born again believer in Christ, they should be. For these words being said by us and practiced, will enable us to grow in grace and in the knowledge of our Lord Jesus Christ.

After all He is the one that, "Endured the cross, despised the shame, and is set down at the right hand of God." (Hebrew 12:2)

Our Lord's position at the Father's right hand is for our benefit as believers in Him. With much fervor and delight it ought to behoove us to believe God who wants us to, "Come boldly to the throne of grace that we may obtain mercy and find grace to help in time of need." (Hebrews 4:16)

We that believe God can find this help of the Father, by the Son, through the Holy Ghost when we come to Him.

O friends today, let us as never before act as if we believe God. The Apostle Paul was no different than us, if we can demonstrate the same belief in God that he had.

Paul was a man of like passions as we are, and could

say when adversity arose in his life "I Believe God." Can you and I imitate him? Yes we can if we can accept the word of God as factual and not fictitious.

I have done my best in our last messages to not only preach about believing God, but also to practice what I believe about Him.

The series we have embarked upon in our last five messages have been about, "Jesus Christ and The Way He Did It." Our discourses have been about His Pre-Existence, His Pre-Incarnation, His Incarnation, Why He was incarnated and our last disquisition was about His character.

In setting forth our Lord's character we set aim on His compassion. We found out that our Lord Jesus showed compassion on the lost, the hungry, the sick, and a demon possessed man of Gadarea. As our Lord showed compassion so must His children whom He has called out of the world.

Another aspect of our Lord's character of which we will focus is "His courage." The word in its original is eparre-siasametha (ep-ar-hray-see-ahs-ah-meh-tha) which is to be bold or daring. It means to speak boldly and freely; to speak out and to speak publicly without fear. Far too many of us fail to witness for Christ because we fear ridicule, embarrassment, mockery, and persecution. That makes us secret believers of Christ instead of bold witnesses for Him.

O friends today, there should be no more Joseph's of Arimathea who was a secret disciple in the days of Jesus, but we should be undaunted in telling the good news to others about the Christ.

The Bible says, in various places about other believers which had courage. The Lord through Moses told Israel, "Be strong and of good courage, fear not nor be afraid of them….. (Deut. 3:6)

"Have not I commanded thee? Be strong and of good courage; be not afraid, neither be thou dismayed." (Joshua 1:9)

Our Lord and Saviour do not require anything of us that He was not Himself.

Is that too much that the Lord requires when He ask us to have courage? Not at all. For like the leader, so ought be the followers.

Why bear the name Christian and we not strive to be like the Christ. It's like Alexander the Great told his namesake, "Either be like me or get rid of the name."

Christian friends, we must as never before take courage for this day and hour, when much cowardice is being portrayed.

M. L. King Jr. said concerning courage. "Courage is an inner resolution to go forward in spite of obstacles and frightening situations; cowardice is a submissive surrender to circumstance. Courage breeds creative self-affirmation; cowardice produces destructive self- abnegation. Courage faces fear and thereby masters it; cowardice represses fear and is thereby mastered by it."

Aren't you and I elated today that cowardice did not hinder our Lord from doing the things He left glory to do.

Nothing and I mean nothing prohibited Him from fulfilling His purpose for mankind.

Let us examine some of the areas of which our Lord took courage.

I. His First Recorded Sermon

> The Bible says, "And He came to Nazareth, where He had been brought up; and as His custom was, He went into the synagogue on the Sabbath day and stood up to read." (Luke 4:16)

> Our Lord read Isaiah 61:1-2, "The Spirit of the Lord is upon me, because he hath anointed me to preach the gospel to the poor; he hath sent me to heal the broken hearted, to preach deliverance to the captives, and recovering of sight to the blind, to set at liberty them that are bruised. To preach the acceptable year of the Lord."

> Because of our Lord's courageousness in declaring the word to his hometown, "Many wondered at the gracious words which proceeded out of his mouth. And they said, is not this Joseph's son?" (Luke 4:22) This brought about our Lord's declaration, "No prophet is accepted in his own country." (Luke 4:24)

> These words along with what our Lord uttered about Elijah being sent to the widow of Zarephath and how Naaman the Syrian had been healed by Elisha, that those in the synagogue were filled with wrath, and rose up, and thrust Him out of the city, and led Him

to the brow of the hill on which their city was built that they might cast Him down headlong, "But He, (Jesus) passing through the midst of them, went His way." (Luke 4:25-30)

Our Lord's courageous words brought about His hometown wanting to kill Him. Notice it was not the bootleggers, drug addicts, alcoholics, gamblers, nor robbers that wanted to take His life, but the religious leaders.

How sad it was for a hometown boy to be treated so bad by those that really knew Him.

What really amazes me and I am sure others is how a preacher that everyone knows is teaching, preaching and living the life can be rejected; and here comes a Joe Blow no one knows and folk flock to and say, "Child, I have never heard anyone like him."

Again how true are the Lord's words, "No prophet is accepted in His own country."

Though our Lord was not accepted, it should behoove us to know that the same thing will happen to us, if we are true to our calling.

Mankind has not changed and will not change in that he still wants smooth things spoken to him.

We must have courage to speak in spite of the consequences. Every disciple of Christ that has, is or ever will be, must have the courage to speak the

Lord's words and not our own. We must never bow to the pressures of society.

Ernest Hemingway said, "Courage is grace under pressure." As our Lord told Jeremiah, "Be not dismayed at their faces." (Jeremiah 1:17b) so is He saying to us.

As the Lord Jesus had courage to proclaim the word at Nazareth, so has He given me the courage to expound His sayings.

Another area of which our Lord took courage was:

II. At The Two Cleansings of the Temple

Both of these instances are recorded in John 2:13-17 and St. Matthew 21:12-16

What courage our Lord displayed at both of these situations. It's believed that the first occasion was at the beginning of His ministry, while the second one was in His final week before Calvary's cross.

Our Lord saw in the temple those who were selling oxen, sheep and doves. The Bible says, "He made a scourge of small cords and drove them all out of the temple, and the sheep, and the oxen; and poured out the changers money, and overthrew the tables.

And said unto them, it is written, my house shall be called the house of prayer, but ye have made it a den of thieves." (Matt. 21:12-13)

These Jews were in the Court of the Gentiles, one of the four courts in the temple, with the others being the Court of the Women, the Court of the Israelites and the Court of the Priests.

In this Court of the Gentiles two kinds of trading were going on, (1) The business of money-changing and (2) The selling of doves which were worse.

In both instances they were making large profits out of it. No great harm would have been done if the prices for the doves had been the same inside and outside the temple, but a pair of doves could cost as little as 4 pence inside the temple.

There is little wonder that our courageous Lord overthrew the tables of the money changers and drove them out.

Another area in our Lord's ministry in which He showed courage was

III. In Risking His Life To Raise Lazarus

This is recorded in St. John 11. Our Lord knew Lazarus was sick but He remained in Jerusalem two days before His departure to Bethany. "Then, after that, saith He to His disciples, Let us go into Judaea again." His disciples said unto Him, "Master, the Jews of late sought to stone thee; and goest thou there again?" Here our Lord showed His disciples that He must take courage and go to Bethany that Lazarus might be raised from the dead.

There comes a time in the life of the believers when we must do what the Lord wants done, in spite of death threats from the opposition.

You remember how the Apostle Paul was warned by believers and the prophet Agabus not to go to Jerusalem. But the preacher said, "What mean ye to weep and to break mine heart? For I am ready, not to be bound only but also to die at Jerusalem for the name of the Lord Jesus." (Acts 21:13)

Shadrach, Meshach, and Abednego had their lives threatened by Nebuchadnezzar and their response was, "O Nebuchadnezzar we are not careful to answer thee in this matter. If it be so, our God, whom we serve, is able to deliver us from the burning fiery furnace, and He will deliver us out of thine hand, O king. But if not, be it known unto thee O king; that we will not serve thy gods, nor worship the golden image which thou hast set up." (Daniel 3:16b-18)

When liberty was offered to John Bunyan, then in prison, on condition of him abstaining from preaching he consistently replied, "If you let me out today, I shall preach again tomorrow."

I'm reminded of Rev. T. J. Johnson whom I honored and respected as a man of God, how that on one occasion in Livingston where I was born and reared, that a white brother came to one of our night services. He told Rev. Johnson not to sing one song nor pray a prayer. Rev. Johnson crossed his legs, sung a song and prayed. That white brother who made the threat went home and was killed by his son.

We must be cognizant that even though our lives are threatened, we must not fear dying, because it is our gain. "For to live is Christ, and to die is gain." (Philippians 1:21)

Our Lord also had courage in:

IV. Condemning the Pharisees

Nowhere else in sacred history (The Bible) nor in secular history will you read a more scorching sermon than the one our Lord Jesus gave unto these religious leaders.

Our Lord had the courage, as well as the boldness to set forth the truth of God to this group. Hear his blistering words to them.

"But woe unto you, scribes and Pharisees, hypocrites! For ye shut up the kingdom of heaven against men, for ye neither go in yourselves, neither suffer them that are entering to go in." (St. Matthew 23:13)

"Ye blind guides, who strain at a gnat, and swallow a camel. Woe unto you, scribes and Pharisees, hypocrites! For ye make clean the outside of the cup and of the platter, but within they are full of extortion and excess. Woe unto you, scribes and Pharisees, hypocrites! for ye are like unto whited sepulchers, which indeed appear beautiful outward, but are within full of dead men's bones, and of all uncleanness. Ye serpents, ye generation of vipers, how can ye escape the damnation of hell?" (St.

Matthew 23:24-25; 27; 33)

Must we condemn the things that we know are wrong? Yes we must if we are to follow our Lord. For us not to say anything against what we know is against the teaching of the Bible, makes us shirkers.

If we don't stand for something, we will fall for anything. Believe me when I say that the favor of God is upon us that will condemn wrong as our Lord did.

Notice that these were not sinners on the outside, but religious folk on the inside. We must blister these types of people with nothing but the truth as our Lord did. Many folk in our churches are religious, but lost and they need this kind of preaching to them, as the Lord gave these Pharisees.

Conclusion:

Let each of us say, "I Believe God" in the character He displayed by setting forth the courage we all need to please the Holy Father.

It was the Lord's courage that took Him to Calvary for the payment of our sins. He was placed in the grave and stayed three days and three nights, but praise God He arose on the first day for our justification.

We can show gratitude to the Lord by saying the words of the song, "Close To Thee", by Fanny Crosby

"Thou my everlasting portion, more than friends or life to me,

All along my pilgrim journey, Saviour let me walk with thee.

Close to thee, close to thee, close to thee, close to thee; all along

My pilgrim journey, <u>Saviour, let me walk with thee.</u>

Gladly will I toil and suffer only let me walk with thee.

Close to thee, close to thee, close to thee, close to thee;

Gladly will I toil and suffer only let me walk with thee."

Chapter 7
His Love For The World

Introduction

As the Lord God has blessed us to embark upon another message, and as each of us draws nearer to our dying day, what better thing for us to do than to say and act like we believe God.

Each discourse has been about, "I Believe God", and I am thankful to the Lord for carrying us on in this series.

When you and I can see the devastation of places like Indonesia, Thailand, Malaysia, Somalia, Tanzania and Kenya, it should awaken us to the fact of believing God.

With over 150,000 who have lost their lives because of a huge ocean wave caused by an underwater earthquake or a Tsunami, it should behoove us to believe God about these happenings.

With nation against nation, and kingdom against kingdom, along with famines, pestilences and other happenings, it is high time that we believe God.

No one can believe God for you. It is not a collective thing, but an individual one. I can't believe God for my wife and family, they must believe Him for themselves.

I can't believe God for you my friends, you must believe Him. The question posed to you this day is a fair one, "Do you believe God?"

The Bible doesn't say here in Acts 27:25, "That the captain of the ship, the centurion, nor the crew, on whether or not they believed God, but it does say that Paul the Apostle believed Him.

With much preparation and perspiration I have tried to set forth to you church that I believe God.

In our last dissertations we set forth to you about "Jesus Christ and the Way He Did It." Our focus was His Preexistence, His Pre-incarnation, Our Lord's Character as set forth in His Compassion and the last one on His Courage.

This morning again in reference to His Character we will take aim at Our Lord's Love (1) For His Father, (2) For His Disciples, (3) For Little Children, (4) Certain Close Friends, and (5) The City Jerusalem. Next week, if the Lord tarries we will focus on His Love for the World.

I. For His Father

> There is no way that the Lord Jesus Christ could have loved His disciples, little children, His close friends, the City of Jerusalem, nor the world had He not first loved His Father.

> Nothing and I mean nothing He ever did was apart from His Father. The Lord Jesus never did anything, nor took on any task without the consent of His Father.

> Of their relationship, hear what the Christ had to say,

"But that the world may know that I love the Father; and as the Father gave me commandment, even so I do." (St. John 14:31)

From this text we can readily see that our Lord was not independent; nor self-reliant, but one who always had connection with His Father.

Throughout the gospel accounts we can see the Father endorsing everything that the Son did. After our Lord had been baptized by John in the Jordan River, the Father spoke from heaven and said, "This is my beloved Son in whom I am well pleased." (St. Matthew 3:17)

On another occasion when our Lord Jesus was addressing His disciples concerning His crucifixion He said, "Now is my soul troubled; and what shall I say; Father, save me from this hour. But for this cause came I unto this hour. Father glorify thy name. Then came there a voice from heaven, saying, I have both glorified it, and will glorify it again." (St. John 12:27-28)

I need to pause right here and pull off my shoes for the Father's endorsement of all that His Son did.

To make application, how sad it is when an earthly son will go his own way instead of seeking the advice of his father.

To take it a little farther, how depressing it is to see spiritual children doing any and every thing without any consultation from their spiritual father, or pastor.

O friends today we must believe God and impersonate our Lord's character in His love for His Father. Each of us should strive not just to please ourselves, but the ones that have the oversight of us.

II. He (Our Lord Jesus) Loved His Disciples

Our Lord's love for the Father automatically made Him love His disciples. Often times when I approach ministers, laymen, and others I pose the question, "How have you been treating the Lord?

If one has been treating the Lord right, they will treat others right. Of our Lord's love for His disciples let us hear from the Saviour Himself.

"A new commandment I give unto you, that ye love one another; as I have loved you, that ye also love one another." (St. John 13:34)

How did our Lord prove His love to His disciples? First and foremost He called them from various occupations to follow Him. Some were fishermen, one was a tax collector, etc., but all had the privilege of a lifetime that was to be loved enough to trail our Lord.

Secondly, His love called for them, as-well as us, to not talk love, but be exemplary with it. As our Lord demonstrated it through His sacrifice, so must we.

How brother pastor is your love for those whom the Lord has put in your care?

Do you just love those that love you, or can you be like Jesus and love Judas too.

All of our disciples are not going to be a John, but the Lord will see to all of us having some Judas's to see just how much love we have.

Never try and get rid of the Judas's for they will eliminate themselves. The Lord Jesus loved Judas from day one until the end and notice; that Judas's betrayal led to his own demise.

Again let us who believe God just go on loving the unlovable, even as our Lord did. Not only did the Lord Jesus love His Father and His Disciples, but He also

III. Loved Little Children

The Bible says, "Then were there brought unto Him little children, that He should put His hands on them, and pray; and the disciples rebuked them." But Jesus said, "Suffer (Permit) little children, and forbid them not, to come unto me; for of such is the kingdom of heaven." (St. Matthew 19:13-14)

What a lesson our Lord taught His disciples concerning little children. We are never to abuse or misuse any of them.

What a lover our Lord Jesus was in that He never discriminated, but exhibited the same love for one group as He did the other.

The little children were no exception, for our Lord Himself was a child and I believe Mary His mother rehearsed to Him about the treatment He received as a child.

She no doubt spoke of the shepherds who were watching over their flock by night when the angel told them, "For unto you is born this day a Saviour which is Christ the Lord." (Luke 2:11) How these shepherds made haste to come and see you as a babe lying in a manger. When they had seen you, how they made known abroad the saying which was told them concerning you as a child.

She also probably told Him of the three wise men that came and brought gifts of gold, frankincense, and myrrh to present to Him as a child.

Not to mention old man Simeon who took you in his arms and blessed God and said, "Lord, now lettest thou thy servant depart in peace according to thy word; for mine eyes have seen thy salvation.

And then my Son there was another old lady named Anna which spoke of you to them that were looking for redemption in Jerusalem. (Luke 2:36-38)

Yes the Lord loved little children for He was loved as one. What we must see is that we should love little children as Jesus did.

Many of us will christen little children who have everything, why not be a god parent to some child who is lacking in spiritual guidance, as well as material things.

As Christ was about children, so should we be. In this day and hour there are a number of little children that needs someone to love them.

IV. He Loved Certain Close Friends

Yes our Lord had some close friends whom He loved. The Apostle John was dear to our Lord.

The Bible says, "Now there was leaning on Jesus bosom one of His disciples, whom Jesus loved." (John 13:23)

Also in John 11:5 the Bible again says, "Now Jesus loved Martha, and her sister (Mary), and Lazarus.

What love our Lord had for these brothers and sisters, which teaches us that you may have friends, but there are some who just are closer than others.

Is that to say that our Lord didn't love others, but John, Lazarus, Mary, and Martha? No it just teaches us that some just became nearer and dearer to His heart than others.

The same applies to the children of the Most High God who will witness the same. We may have many acquaintances in life, but friends will be few.

Let us cherish and thank God for the few we have.

The great Greek philosopher Aristotle posed the question, "What is a friend? His response was, "A single soul dwelling in two bodies."

Did you all get that, "A friend is a single soul dwelling in two bodies?" Friendship is like a bank account, you can't continue to draw on it without making deposits.

You can readily see how the Bible speaks of the husband and wife, that two shall be one flesh. I know we may have other friends, but aside from Jesus, our spouse ought to be our best friend.

The Bible speaks of the friendship that the Lord had with Abraham. It says, "Abraham believed God and it was imputed unto Him for Righteousness: and he was called the Friend of God." (James 2:23)

David and Jonathan had the Lord's kind of friendship. Twice in I Samuel 18: 1 & 3 the Bible says, "Jonathan loved David as his own soul."

David's reply to Jonathan's friendship is in II Samuel 1:25-27. Hear the king in his eulogy of his friend. "I am distressed for thee, my brother Jonathan: very pleasant hast thou been to me: thy love to me was wonderful, passing the love of women."

My friend this day that's the kind of friendship these two had for each other.

The homosexual gang tries to take this scripture to justify their illicit actions, but there was nothing funny about David and Jonathan's relationship. It was one that will go down in history as a true and **bona-fide** friendship.

Let us the church of the living God awaken to the fact that our Lord Jesus wants to be our friend. How can this be? Allow the Lord to answer this question. "Ye are my friends, if ye do whatsoever I have command you." (John 15:14)

If you are having a hard time getting or finding a friend, start now obeying the Lord, and you can become His friend.

For in being His friend, you have one that sticketh closer than a brother. (Proverbs 18:24b)

You also have one as the song says, "Who bears our sins and griefs." One who can take care of our trials and temptations, along with the trouble we encounter. We can take it all to our friend in prayer.

"Can we find a friend so faithful who will all our sorrows share? Jesus knows our every weakness. Take it to the Lord in prayer."

No wonder the Mississippi Mass Choir can sing, "It's Good to Know Jesus." We need to know Him because He wants to be our loving close friend. The question remains, "Do you and I want to be His?" Finally for this message on our Lord's character in the aspect of His love, let us take aim at

V. His Love For The City of Jerusalem

>Though our Lord visited many cities while He tabernacled on earth, yet none was as dear to His heart as the city of Jerusalem.
>
>Hear our Lord's bewailment and blubbering of this sacred city. "O Jerusalem, O Jerusalem, thou that killest the prophets, and stonest them which are sent unto thee, how often would I have gathered thy children together, even as a hen gathered her chickens under her wings, and ye would not." (Matthew 23:37)
>
>Our Lord truly loved this place because He blessed David to capture it from the Jebusites and it was centrally located between the Northern and Southern tribes. It became the capital city.
>
>It, Jerusalem was believed to be Salem, a city ruled by Melchizedek, the king to whom Abraham gave tithes to. (Genesis 14:18)
>
>Jerusalem is also where our Lord had Solomon to build that magnificent temple. Jerusalem, where Nebuchadnezzar and the Babylonian army ravaged the city, carried the inhabitants like Daniel, Shadrach, Meshach, and Abednego into captivity, destroyed the temple and the walls surrounding it.
>
>Jerusalem, the place where our Lord made His triumphal entry, whereby the multitude spread their garments and others cut down branches from the

trees and spread them in the way crying, "Hosanna to the Son of David: Blessed is He that cometh in the name of the Lord; Hosanna in the highest. (Matthew 21:9)

Jerusalem is the place where He cleansed the temple of the money changers, and them that sold sheep and oxen.

Jerusalem, where he told Nicodemus, "Ye must be born again," where He cursed the fig tree, replied to the questions of the religious leaders, gave the parable of the two sons, of the householder, and of the marriage feast.

It is also the place of the tribulation and great tribulation, the second coming, the parable of the ten virgins, the talents and the judgment of the Gentiles.

Jerusalem, where our Lord was anointed by Mary for His burial, where He washed the disciple's feet, ate the Passover meal, partook of the Lord's Supper, denied by Peter, betrayed by Judas and arrested, crucified, buried, and resurrected.

Jerusalem, the place where our Lord will return during His second coming.

O how He loved this city which in the end rejected Him, but His deep love of it stayed with our Lord.

As our Lord wept over Jerusalem for its wickedness, so is He weeping over our condition.

In our cities we are condoning homosexuality, gambling, adultery, and every known sin as the rights of the people and are forgetting about the one who is against them!

O America and other countries we had better stop now, for it is praying time, and the sun is almost down.

For our Lord's weeping over our cities will end and the love He has for us will come to a close, so let us awaken to the fact that as He wanted Jerusalem to repent, so does He want us to.

Let us remember, "Righteousness exalteth a nation, but sin is a reproach to any people." (Proverbs 14:34)

Conclusion:

Praise be to the Father, Son, and Holy Ghost for our Lord's character of love. He loved His Father, He loved his disciples, He loved certain close friends, He loved little children, and he loved the city of Jerusalem. Let us church accept His love for us.

Chapter 8

God's Love

Introduction

The Holy Father through His Son, by the Holy Ghost brings us to another message on these three words, "I Believe God."

Thanks be to the trinity for every message in this series, for the words spoken in the text set forth how one man Paul stood in the midst of a catastrophic event.

The occasion was a tempestuous storm name Euroclydon that appeared on the Mediterranean Sea as Paul and 275 others sailed to Rome.

It was a dark hour on the ship, but light sprang out when this great apostle said, "Wherefore sirs, be of good cheer for I believe God that it shall be even as it was told me."

Have not the same Lord told us many things in His word from Genesis 1:1 to Revelation 22:21 of which He wants us to believe.

But many of us find ourselves not believing God because we will not take Him at His word. Failing to take God at His word by not rightly dividing it proves unequivocally, that we don't believe God.

Many of us find ourselves believing God when it's to our advantage and what we want to hear, but when it's to our disadvantage or something we don't want to hear or accept, we immediately say, "God didn't mean it that way.

As plain as the Bible is on Gambling, Abortion, Women Preachers, Tattoos, Worldly Dancing, Marriage, Salvation, Homosexuality, Hell, and other things, we readily say, "That was for that day and not ours."

I'm afraid today many of us in Christendom cannot say emphatically, "I Believe God", and act on it. Many of us only believe God when it is convenient to do so, for we have the mindset, "I don't want to rock the boat."

Friends when it comes to us believing God, if necessary, let us not only rock the boat, but flip it over. Why? Because so much is being compromised in our day just to get along.

Our problem is we're trying to play on both sides of the fence, which is a disgrace on our part. Hear what the Lord says to us that do so. He that is not with me is against me and he that gathereth not with me scattereth abroad." (Matthew 12:30)

If you and I believe God we are for Him, but if we don't believe Him we are scattering not only ourselves, but those that hear us.

If I could not believe God by declaring the whole counsel of God, I might as well give it all up now and not go any farther. For our Heavenly Father has not, nor ever will be satisfied with those that advocate anything else but the oneness of His word."

In this our message on I believe God, we will conclude with part eight of "Jesus Christ, and The Way He Did It."

Our past expositions were on our Lord's PreExistence, His Pre-Carnation, His Incarnation, Why He was Incarnated, Our Lord's Character, as set forth by His Compassion, His Courage, and His Love.

We have already discussed Our Lord's love for His Father, for His Disciples, His closest friends, the Little Children, and the city of Jerusalem.

Our Lord's culminating love was for the world. The love Our Lord gave to the world is set forth in John 3:16, "For God so loved the world that He gave His only begotten Son, that whosoever believeth in Him should not perish, but have everlasting life."

Here before us are the greatest words ever spoken. I know that secular history records the words of many great statesmen.

Patrick Henry said, "I know not what course others may take, but as for me, give me liberty or give me death."

Dr. M. L. King, Jr. said, "We've got some difficult days ahead. But it really doesn't matter to me now. Because I've been to the mountain top and I have viewed the promise land."

Though the words of these men are quoted and known around the world, yet the words of Jesus are the greatest. For Patrick Henry spoke of himself, as well as Dr. King, but the Lord Jesus's words were the greatest because they included all who would accept them.

Will you my brothers and sisters receive the gift of God's only begotten Son? He is being offered with no strings attached. His only request is that you believe in Him. Is that asking too much my sinner friend for the greatest giver to make you the greatest offer and that being everlasting life?

O how He loved the world and is still in love with it by holding back on His second coming to allow men, women, boys, and girls the chance of a lifetime to be saved from the flames of hell fire.

I'm afraid that too many of us just know John 3:16 by memory and don't have it in our hearts.

Do you my brothers and sisters; especially you young folk, only have John 3:16 in your memory bank and not in your heart?

The Bible says, "It is with the heart, (not with memory) that man believeth unto righteousness; and with the mouth confession is made unto salvation." (Romans 10:10)

Someone has rightly said that John 3:16 is the gospel in a nutshell, that is if we can believe it, we have all of Mathew, Mark, Luke, and John in us.

Our Lord's love for the world in John 3:16 is the perfect answer to the religionists of our day.

> To Atheism, by affirmation "God"
>
> To Agnosticism, by the statement "God so loved"
>
> To Deism, by the declaration "God gave"
>
> To Pantheism, by proclaiming "God so loved the world"
>
> To Eddyism, by the personal pronoun "God gave His Son"
>
> To Unitarianism, by announcing "His only Son"
>
> To Skepticism, by broadcasting "Shall have"
>
> To Legalism, by specifying "Whosoever Believeth"
>
> To Naturalism, by predicting "Shall never perish." Robert T. Boyd

Thanks be to God in Christendom that those of us that believe God have everything we need in John 3:16. Those who have trouble believing God about other doctrinal teachings; stem from us not getting a full grasp of what's said in this great text.

Allow me to say again, "For God so loved the world, that He gave His only begotten Son, that whosoever believeth in

Him should not perish, but have everlasting life." That makes it very special.

There are three things the Lord wants us that believe Him to see in these words before us concerning His love, (1) The Divine Love, (2) The Divine Gift and (3) The Divine Design

I. The Divine Love (For God so loved the World)

    Original Source of Love

    Believe me friends that the love God had was divine, for had it been any other kind we would be most miserable.

    The Lord's love was not eros or sexual love, neither storge or love for family, nor was it phileo or a friendly love, but it was agape love, the only kind of which our Lord produces. His love is not conditional, but unconditional.

    Yes God loved the world, but who makes up the world? It is people, in fact all kinds of people. God loves all because He loves each of us.

    When we say, God so loved the world, we have to break up the mass into its atoms, and to think each atom as being an object of His love.

    Each of us stand out in God's love just as we should do to one another's eyes, if we were on the top of a mountain ridge with a clear sunset sky behind us.

Have you ever realized that when we say, "God loved the world," that it really means, as far as each of us is concerned, He loves me. He loves us all again because He loves each of us.

We my brothers and sisters shall never get all the good of that thought until we translate it, and lay it upon our hearts. It is all very well to say, "O yes! God is love," and it is all very well to say He loves the world. But there is something which is a great deal better to say of which the Apostle Paul uttered, "Who loved me and gave Himself for me." (Galatians 2:20d)

O the <u>depth</u>, <u>height</u>, and <u>width</u> of God's love for the world, and who makes up the world? You and me.

There is little wonder that the saints of old said, He is so wide, you can't go around Him, so low you can't go under Him and so high, you can't go over Him.

Other scriptures that speak of God's love for the world or sinners is John 6:32; Titus 3:4; I John 4:10, "Herein is love, not that <u>we</u> loved God, but that <u>He</u> loved us, and sent His Son to be the propitiation for <u>our</u> sins." II Peter 3:9, "The Lord is not slack concerning His promise, as some men count slackness, but is longsuffering toward <u>us</u>, not willing that any should perish, but that <u>all</u> come to repentance."

The Tsunami tragedy doesn't diminish God's love for mankind and it would do all of us good to know that God still loves the world.

Let none of us downsize the full meaning of God's love again, for He just didn't love us, but He so loved us.

II. The Divine Gift (That He gave His only begotten Son)

> Our heavenly Father's divine love for the world was exemplified in the divine gift of His only begotten Son. The Lord Jesus was given (1) Lovingly, (2) Freely, (3) Wholly.
>
> He could have given nothing else dearer and closer to Him than His only Begotten Son.
>
> We may excel others in kindness; but God's love is such that in its manifestation, it cannot possibly be exceeded.
>
> God's gift in the person of His Son Jesus is incomparable or nothing can compare with it.
>
> God's gift to us is something we should not take for granted. Often you and I get gifts from various ones, some we appreciate and others we don't.
>
> But God's gift of His divine Son is one we should all appreciate and take hold of. The Father gave us the gift Jesus and Jesus turned around and gave His life.
>
> Observe how our Lord Jesus set this forth to

Nicodemus, "As Moses lifted up the serpent in the wilderness, even so must the Son of man be lifted up, That whosoever believeth in Him should not perish, but have eternal life." (St. John 3:14-15)

The Lord Jesus wanted Nicodemus, as well as us to know that the brazen serpent being lifted up in the camps of Israel, brought health and cure within the reach of all who were bitten by serpents.

So would the gift of God in offering up His Son on the cross for our spiritual healing.

Christ was lifted up on the cross and all that look to Him by faith may be saved. Just one faith look is all you need to receive this divine gift. Christ's death is the Christian's life. Christ's cross is the Christian's title to heaven.

How true it is that we deserved death; but Christ, God's gift has died for us. It is true that we are sinners; but Christ has suffered for us. It is true that we are guilty debtors; but Christ has paid our debts with His own blood.

That was the price that the Lord Jesus Christ paid for our sins. It was with His own precious blood. Not only was His blood precious, but it was rare blood, innocent blood, as well as pure blood.

Have you received the gift of God His dear Son, or will you do as multitudes and keep on rejecting Him. Don't you hear the Saviour saying, "Please take my gift, it's yours for the asking."

Please allow me to share with you in the words of the song, "O the Blood", by the New Jersey Mass Choir. I must do this and hope and pray that it will bless your soul and that you would appreciate God' gifts. "O the blood of Jesus, O the blood of Jesus, O the blood of Jesus, it will never lose its power. (The brother said, He thinks He will say it again). O the blood of Jesus, O the blood of Jesus, O the blood of Jesus, it will never lose its power.

> "He was despised and rejected, a man of sorrow acquainted with grief. He was wounded for our transgressions. He was bruised for our iniquities. Still He rose up that third day morning__ He got up with all power in His hand. He has gone back to his Father in glory and He is soon to come again."

> "Everybody sing out O the blood, Sing for the blood of Jesus, It was nothing but the blood___ O ___ O the blood of Jesus. O ___ O the blood of Jesus, it will never lose its power. And I'm glad about it that it will never lose its power__ 365 days, every second, every minute, every hour. Never gonna lose its power. I don't care what you do; it will never lose its power."

Praise God today for the gift of His Son who offered His blood on a hill called Calvary and again that blood will never lose its power. It reaches to the highest mountain, It flows to the lowest valley; It is the blood that gives me strength from day to day.

Again sinner friend and every believer in Christ, "It (The Blood) will never lose its power."

Those of us which believe God have heard of His divine Love, His divine Gift, and finally let us focus finally on

III. The Divine Design

This divine design comes from "Whosoever believeth Him (Jesus) shall not perish, but have everlasting life."

What God wants to do is save all men from perishing. The condition in which He will do this is for one to have faith in His Son.

The Holy Father's divine design for us should receive a ready response on our behalf.

We should never put our Lord on hold when He has so much to offer us. Our Lord has been in the marketing business for a long time and is still soliciting those who will believe in Him.

Your believing in Him will bring about the positive, everlasting life; while the negative will perish for not believing.

Have you ever wondered why the text puts, "Should not perish first?" It is because unless we put our trust in Jesus, we shall certainly perish, and because that certainty of perishing must be averted before we can have everlasting life.

Men do not need to wait until they die before they perish. There are men, women, boys and girls here present who are dead spiritually, and when you come to die, the perishing, which is condemnation and ruin, will only be the making visible, in another condition of life, of what is the fact today.

Dear friends, you do not need to die in order to perish in your sins, and blessed be God, you can have everlasting life before you die.

You can have it now, and there is only one way to have it, and that is to lay hold of Him who is the Life. And when you have Jesus Christ in your heart, whom you will be sure to have if you trust Him, then you will have life__ life eternal, here and now, and death will only manifest the eternal life which you had while you were alive here, and will perfect it in fashions that we do not yet know anything about.

Everlasting life my brothers and sisters is yours for the asking. Our Heavenly Father through His Son, by the Holy Ghost made it so simple.

"God so loved the world that He gave His only begotten Son, that whosoever believe in Him should not perish, but have everlasting life."

Conclusion:

The Lord's plea to each of us is, "Believe me and know that I am the way, the truth and the life; no man cometh unto the Father but by me." (John 14:6)

It is my heart's desire and prayer to God that these messages will enable you to say with the Apostle Paul, "I Believe God."

BIBLIOGRAPHY

Boyd Robert T. – "World's Bible Handbook"

Craft M. Pentz – "Practical Sermon Outlines"

Mark Water – "Christian Quotations"

www.ingramcontent.com/pod-product-compliance
Lightning Source LLC
Chambersburg PA
CBHW071148090426

42736CB00012B/2271